Prayer Keys

by
Mike T. Lacanilao

Back to the Bible
135 West Avenue, Quezon City
P.O. Box 1750 Manila 1099
Philippines

Helping you develop a whole-life pursuit
of Jesus Christ

26,000 printed to date—1997
(1170-247-9M-37)
ISBN 0-8484-0949-X

All Scripture passages are from
the New International Version
unless otherwise noted.

Printed in the United States of America.

To Miriam,
my partner in life and prayer.

Contents

Chapter   **Page**

Foreword 5

1. Why Pray? 7

2. When to Pray 17

3. How to Pray 27

4. What to Pray For 37

Foreword

Never before in the history of the Philippine Church has there been a more exciting time to pray. Churches across the land have been seized by an urgency to pray—through overnight prayer meetings, prayer rallies and dawn watches.

That is why Back to the Bible is launching "The Bible and You" series with *Prayer Keys*.

The country is down. The economy is bad. There is only one answer—God. There is only one key—prayer.

May your prayer life change you into the person God can use to transform your nation upside down.

—Mike T. Lacanilao

"'And when you pray, do not be like the hypocrites, for they love to pray standing in the synagogues and on the street corners to be seen by men. I tell you the truth, they have received their reward in full.

'But when you pray, go into your room, close the door and pray to your Father, who is unseen. Then your Father, who sees what is done in secret, will reward you.

'And when you pray, do not keep on babbling like pagans, for they think they will be heard because of their many words.

'Do not be like them, for your Father knows what you need before you ask him.'"

Matthew 6:5–8

Chapter One
Why Pray?

Of all the spiritual activities men engage in, the most universal must be prayer. Who has never prayed? Even atheists, when in deep distress, have been known to utter fervently, "Save me!" and make all sorts of vows to any god that will listen to them.

Clearly then, many people, if not all of us, pray. But how many of us know the right way to pray?

Prayer is the simplest cry, yet it also can be the most exacting spiritual discipline. For prayer is more than the words we say; it is moving the God of the universe to act on our behalf.

That's why the disciples asked Jesus, "Teach us to pray" (Luke 11:1). We have no record of their having asked Him, "Teach us to preach," or, "Teach us to cast out demons." But recognizing that when Jesus prayed He was in touch with a power greater than any they had ever known, they asked Him, "Teach us to pray."

Jesus' Response

Matthew 6 and Luke 11 record Jesus' answer to the disciples' request. In teaching them the pattern of prayer, He reminded them that because they were part of God's kingdom, they were to pray differently from the rest of the world.

What sets a believer's prayers apart from the prayers of others?

Jesus compared prayer to two other spiritual disciplines: giving and salvation.

The acts of giving and praying have some common qualifications: Both must be done in secret, without any ostentation. Both must be sincere, without any hypocrisy. Both must be simple, free from unnecessary complexities.

Both praying and giving are manifestations of the inner life. Does your giving and praying glorify God?

On the other hand, salvation and praying can be contrasted to each other. While salvation is represented by an open door, praying is represented by a shut door. Salvation begins with a closed door that someone opens to receive the Savior. In Revelation 3:20 Jesus says, "Here I am! I stand at the door and knock. If anyone hears my voice and opens the door, I will come in and eat with him, and he with me."

In contrast, praying begins with an open door that needs to be closed for intimate fellowship with the Father. Look at Matthew 6:6: "'But when you pray, go into your room, close the door and pray to your Father, who is unseen.'"

An insightful man of God wrote: "When the disciples locked the doors, Christ knew He was sure of a welcome. He could not get their ear because of the din and confusion that came through the open door. Closing the door to the world is opening the door to the Master. Don't be afraid of shutting the door. It is the best invitation for the Master to enter."

Why do you need to shut the door to the world when you pray?

Why Should We Pray?

1. We are commanded to pray.

The first compelling reason to pray is that *we are commanded to*. Luke 18:1 tells us, "Then Jesus told his disciples a parable to show them that they should always pray and not give up."

To pray is a command from the lips of the Master and Savior. This thought alone must compel us to obey it. Our Lord further stressed His command in this passage in two ways—by citing a period and telling a parable.

<u>A Period for Prayer</u>

In the preceding chapter, Jesus stated, "'Just as it was in the days of Noah, so also will it be in the days of the Son of Man'" (17:26). Genesis 6 records for us what is was like in the days of Noah. The stench and corruption of sin was such that it reached the high heavens. It distressed even God.

God saw it. "The LORD saw how great man's wickedness on the earth had become, and that every inclination of the thoughts of his heart was only evil all the time" (Gen. 6:5). God saw not only the overt sins committed openly and unashamedly but also the secret sins of the heart and mind.

God felt it. "The LORD was grieved that He had made man on the earth, and his heart was filled with pain" (v. 6). Have you ever realized that *grief* is a love word? We grieve only over those we love.

9

The God of love saw and sensed the sins, and it broke His heart.

God judged it. "So the LORD said, 'I will wipe mankind, whom I have created, from the face of the earth.' . . . So God said to Noah, 'I am going to put an end to all people, for the earth is filled with violence because of them. I am surely going to destroy both them and the earth" (Gen. 6:7, 13).

Our patient, long-suffering God had had enough of unrepentant and abusive mankind. Mark this: God is a God of mercy. He does not take delight in meting out judgment. But His justice and holiness also demand that sin be punished.

"The days of Noah," then, pertain to a period of sin and corruption, no different from our present age. With this setting, Jesus underscored the need for prayer by telling a parable.

A Parable on Prayer

The so-called parable of the persistent widow in Luke 18 has been widely believed to teach the value of importunity, or persistence. Just like the widow, if we pray long enough and persist long enough, God will grow weary and give in to our requests.

But this is a parable of contrast, not comparison. Believers are not likened to the widow. And more importantly, God cannot be likened to the unjust judge. Instead, the contrast is between the unjust judge and our just God, who desires to act on our behalf without any sense of coercion whatsoever.

This is supported by another of Jesus' parables, the one about fatherhood in Luke 11:11–13: " 'Which of you fathers, if your sons asks for a fish, will give him a snake instead? Or if he asks for an egg, will give him a scorpion? If you then, though you are evil, know how to give good gifts to your children, how much more will your Father in heaven give the Holy Spirit to those who ask Him!' "

How can these parables give you more confidence when you pray?

Why should we pray? Because our Heavenly Father, who is loving and just, delights to answer our prayers.

2. We have a contest to win.

The second reason we pray is because *there is a contest to win.* Matthew 26:41 says, "'Watch and pray so that you will not fall into temptation. The spirit is willing, but the body is weak.'"

Two contestants compete within us—the power of prayer versus the pit of temptation; the willingness of the Spirit versus the weakness of the flesh.

Temptation is real and never denied in Scripture. (See 1 Corinthians 10:13 and 1 John 2:16.) Even Jesus faced temptations common to man. The writer of Hebrews said, "For we do not have a high priest who is unable to sympathize with our weaknesses, but we have one who has been tempted in every way, just as we are—yet was without sin" (4:15).

Christ was not exempt from temptation but showed us the key to victory. His secret? "Watch and pray."

What is the secret to victory over temptation?

Perhaps the greatest temptation Jesus experienced was at the Garden of Gethsemane. Knowing fully the intense suffering and humiliation He would go through at the hands of sinful men, He was tempted to give in to the flesh and turn His back on Calvary.

Matthew records Jesus' plea to His Father: "'My soul is overwhelmed with sorrow to the point of death. . . . My Father, if it is possible, may this cup be taken from me'" (26:38–39). Only by prayer and communion was He able to submit to His father: "'Yet not as I will, but as You will'" (v. 39).

Christ wrestled with Satan, the unseen enemy, by intense prayer. He won the victory on Calvary's cross by praying in Gethsemane.

In the Garden, Jesus also showed us the willingness of the Spirit against the weakness of the flesh. Though He pleaded with His disciples to "'stay here and keep watch with me'" (v. 38), three times Jesus found them asleep instead of praying.

Oh, the weakness of the flesh! Jesus knew their frame, as He knows ours. Nevertheless, He does not condone or leave us in our weakness. Instead, He challenges us to support the Spirit, who is willing and desirous to please and obey God. He enjoins us to be more watchful and prayerful.

Yes, there is a contest to overcome, and we shall win it only by prayer.

3. We have a condition to occupy.

The third reason Christians pray is because *it represents a condition to occupy.* Many of us pray; some of us pray more than others; but all of us yearn that our prayers be more powerful.

In James 5:16 we read, "The prayer of a righteous man is powerful and effective." Notice first, what kind of prayer? Powerful and effective, the kind of prayer that moves heaven and extends the hand of God. Then notice, what kind of pray-er (the one who prays)? Powerful and effective prayer can be brought about only by the following right conditions in the lives of those who pray.

First, our lives must manifest faith and faithfulness. James 5:15 talks about the prayer offered in faith, which knows the will of God, asks for it and says, "It shall be done." We can pray with faith when we know something is the will of God.

What conditions for praying effectively should you develop in your life?

Second, we must be in fellowship. James 5:16 also says, "Therefore confess your sins to each other and pray for each other so that you may be healed." So many prayers are weak, hindered and unanswered because of bitterness and grudges in the heart of the person praying.

That broken fellowship can hinder our prayers is vividly shown in the warning given to husbands in 1 Peter 3:7: "Husbands, in the same way be considerate as you live with your wives, and treat them with respect as the weaker partner and as heirs with you of the gracious gift of life, so that nothing will hinder your prayers."

Third, we must fulfill the condition of fitness—not physical fitness, but spiritual fitness. "The prayer of a righteous man is powerful and effective." What kind of a man? A *righteous* man. Why do so many people stay away from prayer meetings? Why do they know so little about prayer? Because they know their sin would make them hypocrites before God.

It is told that during World War II, when bombing became intense in London, a sign in front of one of the churches read, "If your knees knock together, kneel on them." May the difficult days we live in cause us to be prayerful and full of faith. Our decision to support our willing spirits is crucial. Let us support our spirits by being more watchful and prayerful.

Of the three reasons given for you to pray, what motivates you the most?

"Is any one of you in trouble? He should pray. Is anyone happy? Let him sing songs of praise.

"Is any one of you sick? He should call the elders of the church to pray over him and anoint him with oil in the name of the Lord.

"And the prayer offered in faith will make the sick person well; the Lord will raise him up. If he has sinned, he will be forgiven.

"Therefore confess your sins to each other and pray for each other so that you may be healed. The prayer of a righteous man is powerful and effective."

—James 5:13–18

Chapter Two

When to Pray

I like to meditate on what the great men of God say about prayer. For invariably, all the great men of God have been great men of prayer.

James Hudson Taylor was the founder of the Inland China Mission (now Overseas Missionary Fellowship). Having served for 40 years as a missionary in China, he could say boldly, "The sun has never risen upon China without finding me in prayer."

An unknown revivalist once said, "I spend hours in prayer every day, but I live in the spirit of prayer. I pray as I walk and when I lie down. I pray when I awake. The answers are always coming."

And the psalmist David gave this testimony: "Evening, morning and noon I cry out in distress, and he hears my voice" (Ps. 55:17).

Prayer Is an Admission of Need

From the time of our creation, we are dependent on and in need of God. We are physical beings made from dust, yet we possess a spiritual soul.

As spiritual beings, we have a deep capacity for God. This will be met only by maintaining an attitude of prayer every day. However, as physical, emotional and spiritual beings, needs are brought to bear upon us—needs that bring us to our knees in prayer. We are naturally made as needy creatures. And we should be thankful for that!

This seems so strange to many people. Why should we be thankful for the needs we have? For the anxieties and pain we feel right now? For our sad and troubled past?

We have many needs that only the Lord Jesus Christ can meet. If it were otherwise, we would not have turned to Him for salvation as we did. All the trials and sufferings we have gone through and are going through have a purpose in His plan. Isn't that a wonderful truth to hold on to?

Our dependence on Him is illustrated in the analogy of the vine and the branches. Jesus said, "I am the vine; you are the branches. If a man remains in me and I in him, he will bear much fruit; apart from me you can do nothing" (John 15:5).

Which of your needs can only the Lord meet?

When Should We Pray?

While we are to pray at all times (1 Thess. 5:17), there are specific times when we *must* pray.

1. In times of emotional need

Look at James 5:13 again: "Is any one of you in trouble? He should pray. Is anyone happy? Let him sing songs of praises."

Human emotions are varied and changeable. In fact, this verse identifies two emotions that are poles apart. Surely the pendulum swings from one to the other, covering all other emotions in between.

18

The King James Version of the Bible uses the word *affliction*. "Is any among you afflicted?" The immediate and right answer is yes. Who isn't afflicted in some way?

In its broadest meaning, *affliction* refers to the sores and distresses of both body and mind. But since the apostle James specifically refers to physical affliction in verse 14, *affliction* in verse 13 must stand for emotional and mental adversities and hardships.

Everyone, God's people included, go through afflictions of stress and strain. But when afflictions come, how do we react? The way Christians respond sets us apart from the rest of the world.

Our Response to Affliction

There are two ways we can respond to any suffering—the natural way and the biblical way.

When afflictions strike, it is easy and very natural to become bitter and complaining. We become bitter towards ourselves, toward others and ultimately toward God.

How do you respond to problems and pressures?

Even Israel, God's chosen people, fell into this trap. The Book of Numbers relates the following:

> *Now the people complained about their hardships in the hearing of the LORD, and when he heard them his anger was aroused. Then fire from the LORD burned among them and consumed some of the outskirts of the camp.* (11:1)

> *They spoke against God and against*
> *Moses, and said, "Why have you brought*
> *us up out of Egypt to die in the desert?*
> *There is no bread! There is no water!*
> *And we detest this miserable food! Then*
> *the* LORD *sent venomous snakes among*
> *them; they bit the people and many*
> *Israelites died.* (21:5–6)

It is understandable when unbelievers react bitterly to affliction. They do not know God. But when God's people react that way and remain bitter, not only do they miss the blessings that afflictions bring, they are punished.

God does not require us to adopt a stoic, unemotional view to life. He created us with a whole range of emotions with which to respond to life. When you prick your finger, you cry, "Ouch!" This is not old nature or sinful nature. This is simply part of what it means to be human.

Is it wrong for a Christian to feel sorrow or pain?

It is one thing to feel legitimate anguish and sorrow. God wants us to pour it out to Him. However, it is another thing when that intense pain drives a wedge between us and God and slowly turns us bitter against the One who loves us.

A Response That Pleases God

Fortunately, the Bible shows us another way to deal with afflictions. "Is any one of you in trouble? He should pray."

Hard times ought to be prayer times. Not that prayer is to be confined to a time of trouble, but it can be performed to special advantage at such times.

What is your first reaction to hearing bad news?

To this end, God purposely sends afflictions so that we will seek Him early and urgently. Many illustrations in the Bible prove this point.

Manasseh was one of the most wicked kings of Israel. God warned him repeatedly but in vain. As a punishment, the Lord sent the Assyrians to bind him with fetters and take him captive to Babylon. But something good came out of this, as we read in 2 Chronicles 33:12–13:

> *In his distress he sought the favor of the*
> *LORD his God and humbled himself*
> *greatly before the God of his fathers. And*
> *when he prayed to him, the LORD was*
> *moved by his entreaty and listened to his*
> *plea; so he brought him back to Jerusalem*
> *and to his kingdom. Then Manasseh*
> *knew that the LORD is God.*

Hezekiah was one of the good kings of Judah, but this did not exempt him from troubles. Watch how he responded to one situation. After receiving the threats and blasphemous letter of Sennacherib, king of Assyria, Hezekiah "went up to the temple of the LORD and spread it out before the LORD" (2 Kings 19:14).

Jonah is another classic case. Inside the great fish's belly, he cried, "When my life was ebbing away, I remembered you, LORD, and my prayer rose to you, to your holy temple' (Jonah 2:7).

When afflictions draw out groans and complaints, take them to the Lord in prayer.

When the Good Times Come

On the opposite end of affliction is happiness. "Is anyone happy?" (James 5:13). Life, with all its afflictions and problems, is still spiced with joy and mirth. The advice is, sing songs of praise! In distress, pray. In delight, praise!

Paul and Silas prayed and sang hymns to God in prison (Acts 16:25). Prayer and praise are the Christian's normal outlet of feelings. Are we making use of them? We should. With the changeableness of our feelings, it is good to rely on the constants of prayer and praise.

Cultivating a Praising Heart

We must learn not only to be prayerful but praising. A thankful heart knows God's purposes even in seeming defeat. A heart that knows its contentment in God is stable.

With respect to material and emotional needs as well, we ought to say with Paul:

> *I have learned to be content whatever the circumstances. I know what it is to be in need, and I know what it is to have plenty. I have learned the secret of being content in any and every situation, whether well fed or hungry, whether living in plenty or in want. I can do everything through him who gives me strength.*
> (Philippians 4:11–13)

2. In times of physical need

We pray not only in times of emotional need but also in times of physical need. "Is any one of you sick? He should call the elders of the church to pray over him and anoint him with oil in the name of the Lord" (James 5:14).

Sickness visits individuals and families. Ministering to the physically sick and handicapped is endless. Various hospital ministries claim that more people enter the hospital than enter churches.

Could this be the reason why healing campaigns are so popular and well attended? Many people are hurting and need healing.

Two ideas for a biblical healing ministry stand out from this passage. One is human instrumentality. The second is divine intervention.

Human Instrumentality

The person who is sick initiates the call for the elders of the church, who pray for him and anoint him with oil. In biblical days, oil was the medical panacea for various ills. When the 12 disciples were sent out, "they drove out many demons and anointed many sick people with oil and healed them" (Mark 6:13).

Divine Intervention

Oil is likewise the symbol of the Holy Spirit. It is a natural means with supernatural expectations. Pastors can pray, elders and laymen can anoint, professional doctors can prescribe and operate, but only God heals.

Yes, there is human instrumentality, but there also must be divine intervention. I emphasize the words "anoint him with oil in the name of the Lord" (James 5:14) and "the prayer offered in faith" (v. 15).

While unbelievers and ordinary people resort to medicine and surgery without prayer, believers use every good gift and modern medicine, while leaving the healing to the sovereign power of God.

There is no healing that is not divine. Many people are healed in the body only. What a difference it is to be healed in the body and edified in the soul and spirit. That is true healing.

Do you need true healing?

3. In times of spiritual need

We also pray in times of spiritual need. "Therefore confess your sins to each other and pray for each other so that you may be healed" (James 5:16).

Just as emotional and physical needs are many and real, so are our spiritual needs. Though less visible, spiritual needs are as real, if not more pressing.

James prescribes mutual confession and mutual praying. Honest confession maintains the fellowship of the saints. Pride and stubbornness hinder it. What we often hear in courts during litigation, sad to say, is also common in churches: "Not guilty, your honor."

What does James say is needed to maintain the fellowship of the saints?

There is so much dishonesty and hypocrisy. The only remedy for this is honest confession—hard for the pride but always good for the soul. Mutual, open confession should lead to mutual prayer and bearing one another's burden.

In James 5:17, the example of Elijah is cited: "Elijah was a man just like us. He prayed earnestly that it would not rain, and it did not rain on the land for three and a half years." Although many other prayer warriors could have been cited, Elijah was singled out for one reason—he was a man very much like us and subject to passions we have.

But in one sense he was different. In this he is held up as our ideal model: He prayed earnestly. The King James Version renders verse 16 as, "The effectual fervent prayer of a righteous man availeth much." Elijah had a right relationship with God. That spells power.

As humans, we may have the same susceptibilities, same dispositions and same infirmities. But we differ in our fellowship with God. Power in prayer comes out of a quality relationship with God.

"So what shall I do? I will pray with my spirit, but I will also pray with my mind; I will sing with my spirit, but I will also sing with my mind.

"If you are praising God with your spirit, how can one who finds himself among those who do not understand say 'Amen' to your thanksgiving, since he does not know what you are saying?

"You may be giving thanks well enough, but the other man is not edified."

1 Corinthians 14:15–17

Chapter Three

How to Pray

In the previous chapter, we saw that though all of us may pray, not all prayers have the same effect. That's because there are God-honoring and God-dishonoring modes of prayer.

I treasure this quote from William Law:

> *It is not the <u>arithmetic</u> of our prayers, how many they are;*
> *nor the <u>rhetoric</u> of our prayers, how eloquent or elegant they are;*
> *nor the <u>geometry</u> of our prayers, how long they may be;*
> *nor the <u>music</u> of our prayers, how melodious or sweet-sounding they are;*
> *nor the <u>method</u> of our prayers, how orderly they may be.*
> *Which God cares for: <u>the fervency of the Spirit</u> is that which availeth much.*

What should characterize our prayers?

Many instances of prayer in the Scriptures serve as inspirations and models for us. Four such instances from the New Testament give us important principles on how God wants us to pray.

We ought to pray with the understanding of Paul, the style of Epaphras, the example of James and in the Spirit of God.

The Understanding of Paul

Paul's prayer understanding is stated in 1 Corinthians 14:15: "I will pray with my spirit, but I will also pray with my mind; I will sing with my spirit, but I will also sing with my mind." He is saying that when we pray, it must be with clarity and comprehension.

The Context

This verse is in the section of 1 Corinthians where Paul discusses spiritual gifts. Beginning with chapter 12, he talks about the gifts that are given to maintain unity within the diversity of the church. He concludes the chapter by showing us the most excellent way—the way of love.

The 13th chapter contains Paul's famous treatise on love. He elevates love as the greatest among the three virtues (faith, hope and love). Paul then begins chapter 14 with a statement linking the previous chapter to the present chapter. He says, "Follow the way of love" (v. 1).

Two Illustrations

Using his previous discussion as a foundation, Paul talks about the use of spiritual gifts in the context and profit of the church as a community. He elucidates this by citing two areas of the human arts, namely music (vv. 7–8) and speech (v. 9).

Paul mentions some musical instruments—the flute, harp and trumpet—in the context of playing them not for personal pleasure but for public performance or concerts. In public performances, unless notes are clear and correct, people will not understand or be moved to action.

By the same token, Paul talks about speech. A person may be loud and long-winded, but if his words are not clear and understood, it is like he is speaking into the air. Paul drives home a point in verse 15 by asking, "So what shall I do?"

As with music and speech, our prayers, especially in public, must be said with understanding and comprehension. Why? Because people praying with us can say "amen" with sincere agreement only if they understand us. Prayers said with understanding and in the Spirit should be supported with "amen" either inwardly or audibly. Likewise, singing in the Spirit will be applauded to the glory of God.

Why is it important to pray with understanding?

In private prayer, we don't need to utter a word. Our spirits can simply worship. But when praying publicly, make Spirit-filled prayers clearly and understandably. This is praying with the understanding of Paul.

The Style of Epaphras

Second, we must pray with the style of Epaphras. Paul records Epaphras's prayer life in Colossians 4:12–13:

> *Epaphras, who is one of you and a ser-*
> *vant of Christ Jesus, sends greetings. He*
> *is always wrestling in prayer for you,*
> *that you may stand firm in all the will of*
> *God, mature and fully assured. I vouch*
> *for him that he is working hard for you*
> *and for those at Laodicea and Hierapolis.*

Epaphras was the founder of the church at Colossae. Now in prison, he had a new ministry—the ministry of prayer. Let's observe the manner in which he prayed for his flock.

First, Epaphras prayed in humility. In writing to the Colossians, Paul identified Epaphras as "one of you and a servant of Christ Jesus" (4:12)—not *over* them but *one of* them, not a master but a servant. Epaphras was humble and always willing to serve. Even as a prisoner, he was very useful in the ministry of prayer.

Radio Bible teacher Dr. J. Vernon McGee once narrated receiving a letter from a young preacher who had become paralyzed and could not preach anymore. He wanted to find out how he could still be used of God. McGee answered, "I have a job for you. Pray for me."

If you are taken out of active service, pray for God's other servants. That is His new ministry for you.

Second, Epaphras prayed with hard work. He not only prayed in humility, he also prayed with hard work. He was "laboring fervently in prayer" (KJV), "always wrestling in prayer" (NIV).

How can you attain success in prayer?

Epaphras prayed hard in order to achieve an objective: that the Colossian believers "may stand firm in all the will of God, mature and fully assured" (v. 12).

30

As a prayer warrior, he was hitting a mark. It takes practice and hard work to be a sharpshooter. What is required in sports is required so much more in prayer. The only way we can learn to pray with great effect is to pray diligently. To be great in prayer requires hard work.

Those who want great success in prayer must take great pains in prayer—long hours, early rising, deep concentration. God sees and honors the sacrifices we make in secret.

Third, Epaphras prayed with heat. Paul said of him, "For I bear him record, that he hath great zeal for you (Col. 4:13, KJV). The word *zeal* refers to the warmth, ardor and enthusiasm of Epaphras, and it showed especially in his prayers. There is much casualness in many of our prayers, but Epaphras prayed with absolute zealousness. We can learn much from the style of Epaphras, whose prayers were characterized by humility, hard work and heat.

What can you learn from Epaphras's prayer life?

The Example of James

Third, we can pray with the example of James. "But when he asks, he must believe and not doubt, because he who doubts is like a wave of the sea, blown and tossed by the wind" (James 1:6).

The Epistle of James, written by one of Jesus' disciples, is a book on practical Christian living. It is so practical that some people believe it was written to combat Paul's emphasis on faith. This, however, cannot be possible for two reasons.

First, James wrote his letter around A.D. 45–50. The earliest of Paul's epistles (1 Thessalonians) was written about A.D. 52–56. Therefore, James had nothing to refute, since none of Paul's epistles were written yet.

Second, it must be clear that the theme of James is not works but faith, the same as Paul's themes. The seeming contradiction arises because James emphasizes the visible product of faith, which is works.

One proof of this is in the aspect of prayer. James' teaching on prayer can be an example to us in two areas:

1. James' prayers were with perspiration. Among the 12 apostles, he is known through tradition as the apostle with "camel knees," meaning his knees had become hard and calloused because of so much kneeling in prayer. He spent much time in prayer, shedding copious tears and sweat.

2. James' prayers were with power. When James writes, "But when he asks," he means prayer with power. Jesus Himself speaks of the power of faith in Matthew 17:20: "I tell you the truth, if you have faith as small as a mustard seed, you can say to this mountain, 'Move from here to there' and it will move. Nothing will be impossible for you."

How did James pray?

Towards the end of his epistle, James once more touches on the subject of prayer in 5:15 and describes it as the prayer of faith. The practical prayer of faith—that is an excellent example to us.

The Spirit of God

Finally, we must pray in the Spirit of God. In Ephesians 6:18, Paul says, "And pray in the Spirit on all occasions with all kinds of prayers and requests. With this in mind, be alert and always keep on praying for all the saints."

The sixth chapter of Ephesians is devoted to Paul's description of the full armor of God for the Christian. God makes available for us a complete arsenal for our defense against our enemy, Satan.

Among them are the belt of truth (v. 14), the breastplate of righteousness, the shoes of the gospel of peace (v. 15), the shield of faith (v. 16) and the helmet of salvation (v. 17).

Notice that all the weapons above are for defense, and in particular, for repulsing attacks against the front part of our bodies. There is no protection for the back. Nothing is provided for retreat because a Christian is not to retreat.

Two weapons are for offense: the sword of the Spirit, which is the Word of God (v. 17), and prayer (v. 18). Prayer is not listed as part of the armor of the Christian because it is meant to be a lifestyle, an ongoing activity. It strengthens us so we can use every piece of the armor to our advantage.

Many of us pray, but how many really pray in the Spirit? How many of us consciously acknowledge and beseech the Spirit's leading in our prayers—to start, to direct, to energize, even to end our prayers?

Are prayers offensive or defensive?

We must pray in the Spirit when we engage in all kinds of prayer (public or private, social or solitary, solemn or sudden) with all parts of prayer (confession of sin, petition for mercy and thanksgiving for favors received). Our spirits must be employed in the duty of and in fellowship with the Holy Spirit.

Herein lies the secret of power of prayer: praying with the understanding of Paul, the style of Epaphras, the example of James and in the Spirit of God.

" 'You have heard that it was said, "Love your neighbor and hate your enemy."

'But I tell you: Love your enemies and pray for those who persecute you,

'that you may be sons of your Father in heaven. He causes his sun to rise on the evil and the good, and sends rain on the righteous and the unrighteous.

'If you love those who love you, what reward will you get? Are not even the tax collectors doing that?

'And if you greet only your brothers, what are you doing more than others? Do not even pagans do that?

'Be perfect, therefore, as your heavenly Father is perfect.' "

—Matthew 5:43–48

Chapter Four
What to Pray For

Prayer—talking to our Heavenly Father—can be the most engaging activity Christians ever participate in. Prayer—moving the hand of our Almighty God—can be the most powerful weapon we can ever employ.

Dr. John Stott, the most eminent Bible scholar of our day, said, "Prayer is the greatest force that we can wield. It is the greatest talent that God has given. He has given it to every Christian. What right have we to leave unappropriated or unapplied the greatest force which God has ordained for the salvation and transformation of man?"

What is the greatest thing you have asked the Lord for this week?

As S. D. Gordon pointed out, through prayer we can travel around the world as missionaries and reach out and help:

> *The greatest thing each one of us can do is to pray. If we can go personally to some distant land, still we have gone to only one place. Prayer puts us in direct dynamic touch with a world.*

*A man may go aside today, and shut the
door, and as really spend a half hour of
his life in India for God (or Russia or
China) as though he were there in person.
Surely you and I must get more half
hours for this secret service.*

Scripture enjoins us to pray for several things. Let us begin with the prayer object that perhaps is the hardest and most difficult to undertake.

Pray for the Haters

In Matthew 5:44, Jesus said, "But I tell you: Love your enemies and pray for those who persecute you."

Many people are called to mind by the word *enemy*, but Jesus is talking here about haters, because there is an element of hate in every enemy that leads them to do what they do.

Despite everything, we are told to do the following: Love them, bless them, do good to them and pray for them.

Who comes to mind when you think about those who have something against you?

Love Our Enemies

Loving our enemies is definitely contrary to the world's conduct. The world's attitude is described in verse 43—love our good neighbors and hate our enemies. But as Christians, our Great Peacemaker and Reconciler lifts us to the standard and principles of His kingdom and tells us, "Love your enemies."

Doing this, we are reminded of our past: "When we were God's enemies, we were reconciled to him through the death of his Son" (Rom. 5:10).

Why do you have nothing to boast of over your enemies?

No matter how bad people are, believers are really no different from them. We are all sinners. From our hearts spring the same fleshly passions and self-centered motives that they have. Ephesians 2:1–3 pictures us so well:

> As for you, you were dead in your transgressions and sins, in which you used to live when you followed the ways of this world and of the ruler of the kingdom of the air, the spirit who is now at work in those who are disobedient. All of us also lived among them at one time, gratifying the cravings of our sinful nature and following its desires and thoughts. Like the rest, we were by nature objects of wrath.

But praise be to our God that He condescended to show mercy to us:

> But because of his great love for us, God, who is rich in mercy, made us alive with Christ even when we were dead in transgressions—it is by grace you have been saved. (Eph. 2:4–5)

The bottom line is that we really have nothing to boast of. If not for God's mercy, we would be exactly like the unbelievers, some of us even worse.

Do you know someone you need to forgive and reconcile with? Show kindness to him or her today.

Bless Our Enemies

Because God extends His mercy to us, we owe our enemies a debt of love for His sake. The best formula of love that we can feed them is to share the Gospel of love with them. Thereby, we bless them. "Do not repay evil with evil or insult with insult, but with blessing, because to this you were called so that you may inherit a blessing" (1 Peter 3:9).

Do Good to Our Enemies

Christians are also called to do good to our enemies. It was said of Archbishop Cranmer that the way to make him a friend was to do him an ill turn. What a powerful testimony! That is true Christianity. That is the true spirit of the Savior.

Pray for Our Enemies

We must also pray for those who hate us. It is not new or unusual for saints to be hated and cursed by wicked people. Christ Himself was so treated. If we cannot openly show our love to them, prayer is the best and least ostentatious way to show our love. Go to God on their behalf.

The Biggest Blessing Is Ours

When we love, bless, do good and pray for those who hate us, we realize that we are the ones receiving the biggest blessing. In addition, when we in humility and brokenness start praying for and loving our enemies, a number of things happen.

First, we please God and prove to be His sons. Matthew 5:45 says, "That you may be sons of your Father in heaven. He causes his sun to rise on the evil and the good, and sends rain on the righteous and the unrighteous."

We are sons being conformed to our Father's character in love and kindness. A proof of His kindness is the way He allows the sun to shine on both the evil and the good, and the rain to pour on both the just and the unjust.

Second, we shall be rewarded for loving our enemies. Verses 46–47 say that loving those who love us and greeting only our friends is commonplace. Even the heathen do that. But we are to exercise the Christian spirit to everyone: "If your enemy is hungry, feed him; if he is thirsty, give him something to drink. In doing this, you will heap burning coals on his head" (Rom. 12:20).

We are to melt the hearts of our enemies into friendship and forgiveness.

Have you ever shown favor to an enemy? How did God reward your conduct?

Third, the ability of a Christian to pray for those who hate him perfects him. "Be perfect, therefore, as your heavenly Father is perfect" (Matt. 5:48).

The word *perfect* for a Christian refers to his full development and growth into godliness. As Christians, we must learn to aspire for and desire perfection towards grace and holiness, thereby conforming ourselves to the example of God our Father.

What is the greatest blessing for you when you do good to your enemies?

Pray for the Harvest

We pray not only for the haters but also for the harvest.

> *When [Jesus] saw the crowds, he had compassion on them, because they were harassed and helpless, like sheep without a shepherd. Then he said to his disciples, "The harvest is plentiful but the workers are few. Ask the Lord of the harvest, therefore, to send out workers into his harvest field."* (Matt. 9:36–38)

What is missions? Again I quote Dr. Stott: "It is the activity of God arising out of His very nature. The living God of the Bible is a sending God, which is what missions means." From David Livingstone comes this beautiful thought: "God has an only Son and He was a missionary."

Jesus likened missions to a harvest. There is nothing profound in the analogy He used. This simple illustration was easily understood by city people, although it was strictly a rural context.

Jesus talked about harvest in relation to the laborers. He pointed out that the harvest was ready but the laborers were still not on the job site. What a pathetic disparity!

Before Him was a wide open harvest field of labor opportunities. In contrast, He saw just a handful of laborers, not enough to handle the abundant harvest.

And among the few workers available, some were not even on the work site.

With this situation, what are we to do? Give up in despair and allow the harvest to decay? No, we are told to pray. "'Ask the Lord of the harvest, therefore, to send out workers into his harvest field'" (v. 38). The mightiest weapon of the Church and the highest ministry of the individual believer is to approach God as the Lord of the Harvest.

We all know too well how self-centered our prayers are. We dwell on our personal needs, family needs and church needs, but how often do we pray for Christian workers, Christian organizations and world missions?

As we pray, the Lord recruits and thrusts out. This is His work, but as His children we must also do our part. We must pray for the harvest.

Pray for the Household

We are also commanded to pray for the household.

In his letter to the Colossians, as in his other epistles, Paul wrote to the saints and brethren in the local churches. Wherever Christians are, they are part of the household of God.

Paul expressed his concern for the Colossian Christians. He explained how having heard of their faith, love and hope, he never ceased to pray for them: "For this reason, since the day we heard about you, we have not stopped praying for you and asking God to fill you with the knowledge of his will through all spiritual wisdom and understanding" (Col. 1:9).

No doubt this is a prayer of rejoicing over their spiritual health and success. But it is also a prayer that their spiritual soundness might be maintained.

What marks Paul's relationship to those he discipled?

Paul was praying for the fullness of spiritual wisdom. It is important that believers be endowed with wisdom from on high daily. Paul also prayed for their spiritual walk, that they may have a pleasing walk brought about by seeking God's will and resulting in fruitfulness.

> *And we pray this in order that you may live a life worthy of the Lord and may please him in every way: bearing fruit in every good work, growing in the knowledge of God, being strengthened with all power according to his glorious might so that you may have great endurance and patience.* (Col. 1:10–11)

Paul was also concerned about the Colossians' spiritual weight and worth. Where there is spiritual life, there is need for spiritual strength. We are strengthened and keep our spiritual weight only as we conform our conduct and behavior to God's revealed will.

The prayers we find in the Bible are meant to serve as patterns for us when we pray for fellow Christians. Too many times we limit ourselves to praying for their material and physical needs. Let's follow the apostle Paul's example by praying for people's spiritual growth.

Pause now and pray through Colossians 1:9–11 for yourself and another believer. Make a habit of using Scripture in your prayers.

Pray for the Hierarchy

Finally, we are enjoined to pray for the hierarchy.

> *I urge, then, first of all, that requests, prayers, intercession and thanksgiving be made for everyone—for kings and all those in authority, that we may live peaceful and quiet lives in all godliness and holiness.* (1 Tim. 2:1–2)

When Paul wrote this, the bloody and cruel Nero was ruler over the Roman Empire. Paul was in prison, a victim of injustice, yet he strongly solicited prayers for kings, whoever they were. He knew that any government is better than no government at all.

Civil government is a gift from God, and we have a duty to pray for it so that we might live a quiet and peaceable life in all godliness and honesty. Many of us fall short in this responsibility of remembering and praying for our government.

Pray for your hierarchy—for kings and presidents, whether in power, deposed or in exile, and for all those in authority. God has put them in seats of power and authority. He uses even evil, pagan kings—His enemies—for His purposes (Isa. 45:1–6).

As you read the newspaper each day, bring pressing national and local concerns to the Lord.

Our Response

Every revelation of God calls for a response. Every promise is set in operation by a condition met.

Our Heavenly Father invites us to a deeper experience of His power in the inner life through prayer. He bids us to open our prayer closet and go in. He bids us to put our trust in His promises.

What will your response be?